Snyder · Higgi

COMPREHENSIVE GUITAR METHOD

CONTENTS

Alfred Publishing Co., Inc.
16320 Roscoe Blvd., Suite 100
P.O. Box 10003
Van Nuys, CA 91410-0003
alfred.com

ISBN-10: 0-89898-701-6
ISBN-13: 978-0-89898-701-0

How To Use This Book

The COMPREHENSIVE GUITAR METHOD is a new approach to the instrument which provides for the development of a variety of styles and techniques. The course presents a balance of guitar instruction bringing into play related areas such as music theory, classical guitar and folk songs.

As a student of the guitar, it is important to remember that this instrument has a long and honorable history and has responded to the extreme demands of many fine musicians. The ability to play a few chords does not begin to realize the potential of the guitar as a means of musical expression. Properly studied, the guitar is capable of opening the door to an exciting world of musical experience for you. This book represents a first step in the exploration of this vast realm.

As you practice: (1) begin with the most basic technique in each section; (2) balance your work with portions taken from each section of this book. Learn the first chord examples while you learn the first basic strums, along with the fundamentals of notation. Apply your knowledge immediately to one of the songs corresponding to your level of study. Gradually progress through the book in this manner and you will be amazed at your rapid development.

ABOUT THE GUITAR

This section explains the parts of the guitar, how to hold the guitar and how to tune the guitar. Be familiar with all terminology as it relates to the instrument. Check your position occasionally and make corrections as needed. Work to develop your ability to differentiate between levels of pitch in order to play with the proper intonation (play in tune). The ability to tune the guitar may seem difficult, however by training yourself to "listen" you begin to develop this facility.

GUITAR CHORDS

Beginning with the Key of D, learn I, IV, V7 chords. Apply these chords to the songs in the song section using the suggested strums. To play songs in more difficult keys, you must learn to play bar chords. Three forms of the bar chord are given in this book.

Fingers may become sore when beginning. They will gradually toughen up and increase in flexibility and dexterity as you progress in your studies.

GUITAR STRUMS

Starting with the Folk Strums, begin to develop right hand technique. Right hand technique develops slowly and is difficult to apply to songs in the beginning. Keep the strums simple and stress the development of the left hand (ability to play chords) before progressing to the more difficult Finger Strums.

MUSIC NOTATION

Prepare for this section by learning the music signs and symbols given on page 28-29 and by practicing the exercises given on page 30. The ability to read music is an important part of being a musician. An interesting approach to note reading and the understanding of written music can be found in the notation section of this book.

SONGS

The Song Index indicates the key and the difficultly level of each of the songs. Suggested strums correspond generally to the strum section. Songs in a variety of keys have been included in the Song Section.

About The Guitar

For the finger-style (classical) approach of this course, the authors recommend an acoustical guitar with nylon strings, an open peg box and 19 frets.

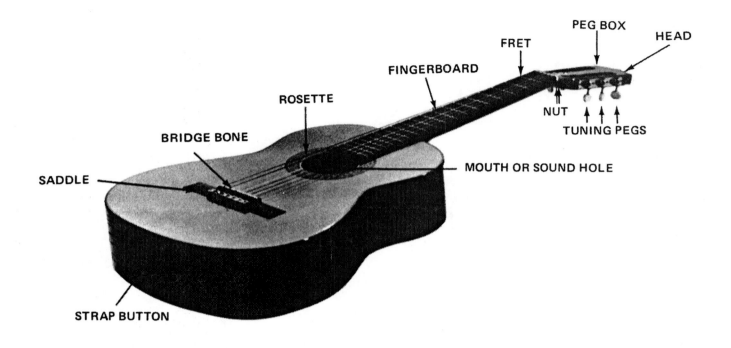

fig. 1

HOLDING THE GUITAR

FOLK METHOD — The folk method is a compromise of the classical guitar method of holding the guitar.

IN A SITTING POSITION:

1. place the side of the guitar on the right thigh.

2. slightly tilting the guitar, hold it against your body.

3. hold the neck of the guitar at about a 10 to 15 degree angle to the floor (upward) — SEE FIGURE 2.

4. place the forearm on the edge of the guitar just above the saddle (wrist and finger action will execute the various strums — not arm movement).

fig. 2

NOTE: Other commonly acceptable methods of holding the guitar may be permitted; however, give PRIMARY ATTENTION to the placement of the RIGHT FOREARM on the top of the guitar.

Tuning the Guitar

4

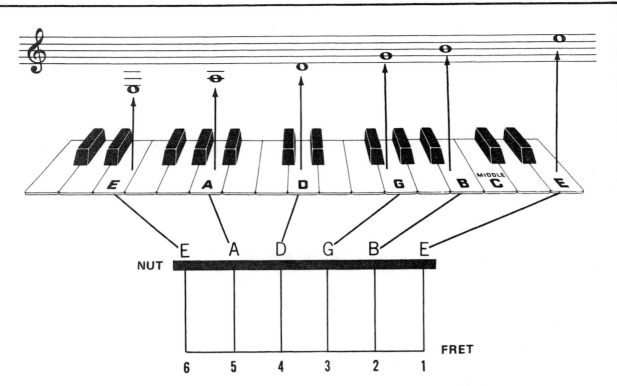

The guitar may be tuned to the piano. The six guitar strings are shown above as their pitch corresponds to the note on the piano. The notes as they are written in the staff are given directly above the piano keys. Guitar notation *sounds* an octave lower than written.

MAKE THE NECESSARY TUNING ADJUSTMENTS BY TIGHTENING STRINGS TO RAISE PITCH AND LOOSENING STRINGS TO LOWER PITCH.

Using the "relative pitch" method the guitar strings are tuned to each other starting with the low E (sixth) string.

1. Estimate the pitch of the lowest string (sixth).

2. Press 6th string at the 5th fret to get pitch of 5th string.

3. Press 5th string at the 5th fret to get pitch of 4th string.

4. Press 4th string at the 5th fret to get pitch of 3rd string.

5. Press 3rd string at the 4th fret to get pitch of 2nd string.

6. Press 2nd string at the 5th fret to get pitch of 1st string.

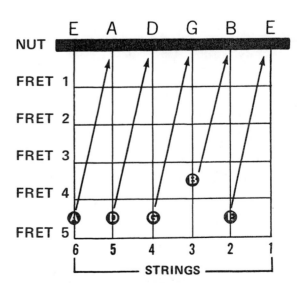

NOTE: Approach the tuning of each string by purposely going below the pitch and, while you pluck the open string with your thumb, slowly turn the tuning peg with your left hand.

F.I. 2287

Guitar Chords

The guitar utilizes two basic types of chord formations: 1) open string chords; 2) bar chords. Standard diagrams will be used to pictorially describe each chord.

Chord Diagrams

Each diagram represents the fingerboard of the guitar and shows the placement of the fingers, fingerings to be used and upon which strings the ROOT (primary bass note) and the 5th (alternate bass note) are located. fig. 1.

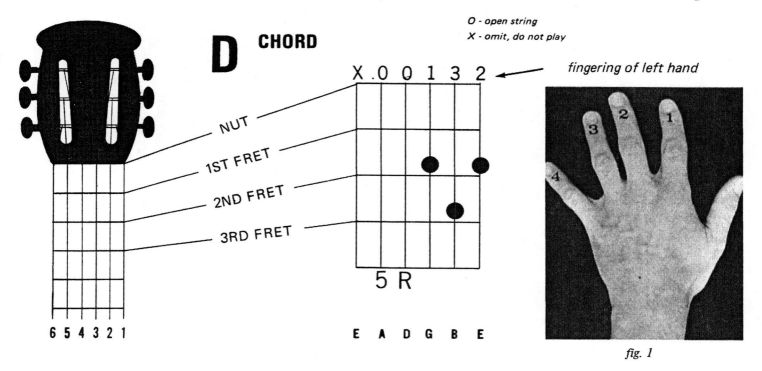

fig. 1

Left Hand Position

FINGERS - Put the fingers as close to the frets as possible without actually touching the fret. Place the fingers on their tips (nails must be short) to avoid touching adjacent strings. Press down firmly. fig. 2 and 3.

THUMB - Place the thumb on the back of the neck slightly past the middle. The thumb is opposite the 1st finger (this will vary slightly with some chord formations). fig. 4

fig. 2

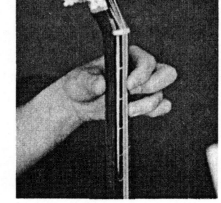
fig. 3

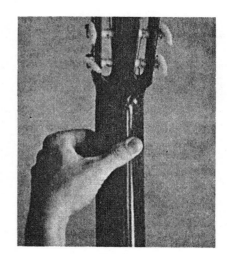
fig. 4

♪ NOTE: Do not allow the palm of the hand to touch the neck of the guitar.

Open String Chords

Open string chords are those which contain a maximum of open strings and a minimum of depressed strings. Memorize the I, IV, V7 chords in the following keys and apply them to the songs. Song Section — page 43.

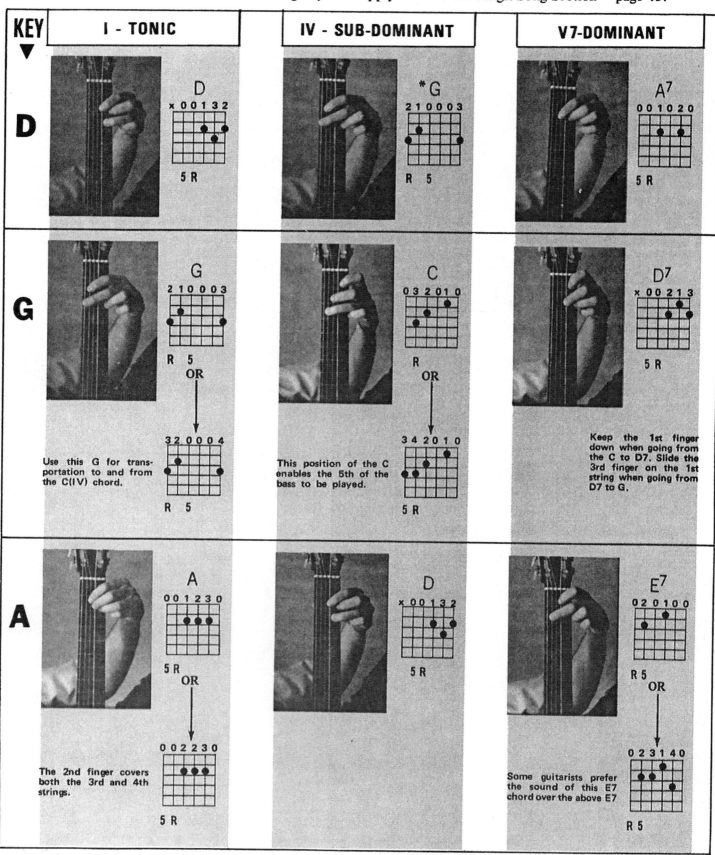

♪ NOTE: *For simplified version of G chord, see page 8.

Open String Chords

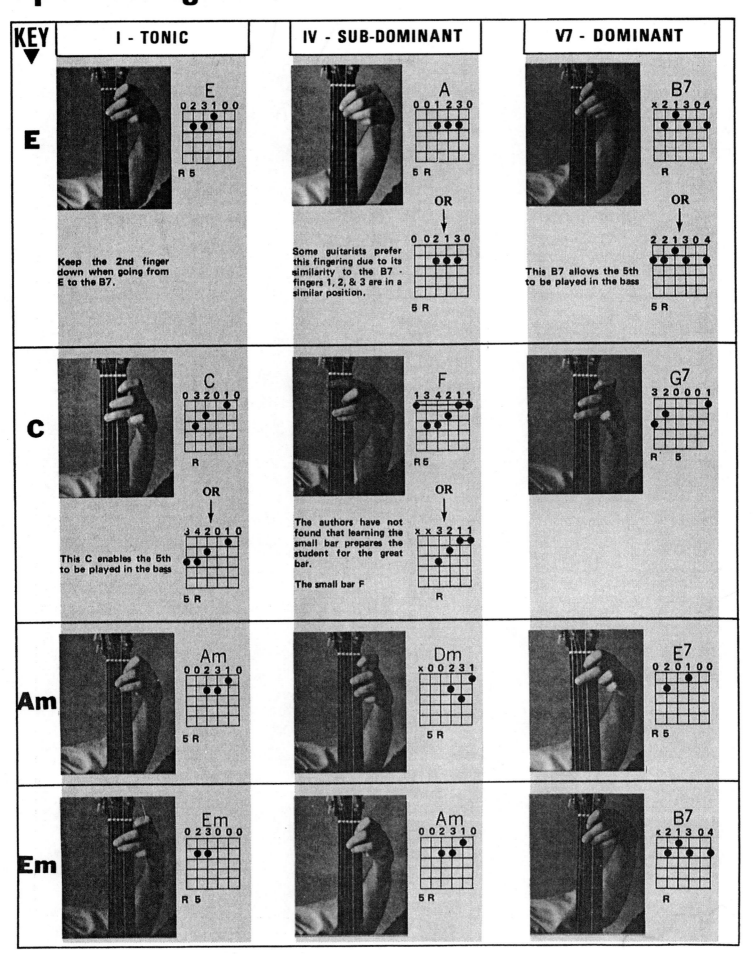

KEY ▼	I - TONIC	IV - SUB-DOMINANT	V7 - DOMINANT
E	E — 0 2 3 1 0 0 — R 5 — Keep the 2nd finger down when going from E to the B7.	A — 0 0 1 2 3 0 — 5 R — OR — 0 0 2 1 3 0 — 5 R — Some guitarists prefer this fingering due to its similarity to the B7 - fingers 1, 2, & 3 are in a similar position.	B7 — x 2 1 3 0 4 — R — OR — 2 2 1 3 0 4 — 5 R — This B7 allows the 5th to be played in the bass
C	C — 0 3 2 0 1 0 — R — OR — 3 4 2 0 1 0 — 5 R — This C enables the 5th to be played in the bass	F — 1 3 4 2 1 1 — R 5 — OR — x x 3 2 1 1 — R — The authors have not found that learning the small bar prepares the student for the great bar. The small bar F	G7 — 3 2 0 0 0 1 — R 5
Am	Am — 0 0 2 3 1 0 — 5 R	Dm — x 0 0 2 3 1 — 5 R	E7 — 0 2 0 1 0 0 — R 5
Em	Em — 0 2 3 0 0 0 — R 5	Am — 0 0 2 3 1 0 — 5 R	B7 — x 2 1 3 0 4 — R

Frequently Used Open String and Simplified Chords

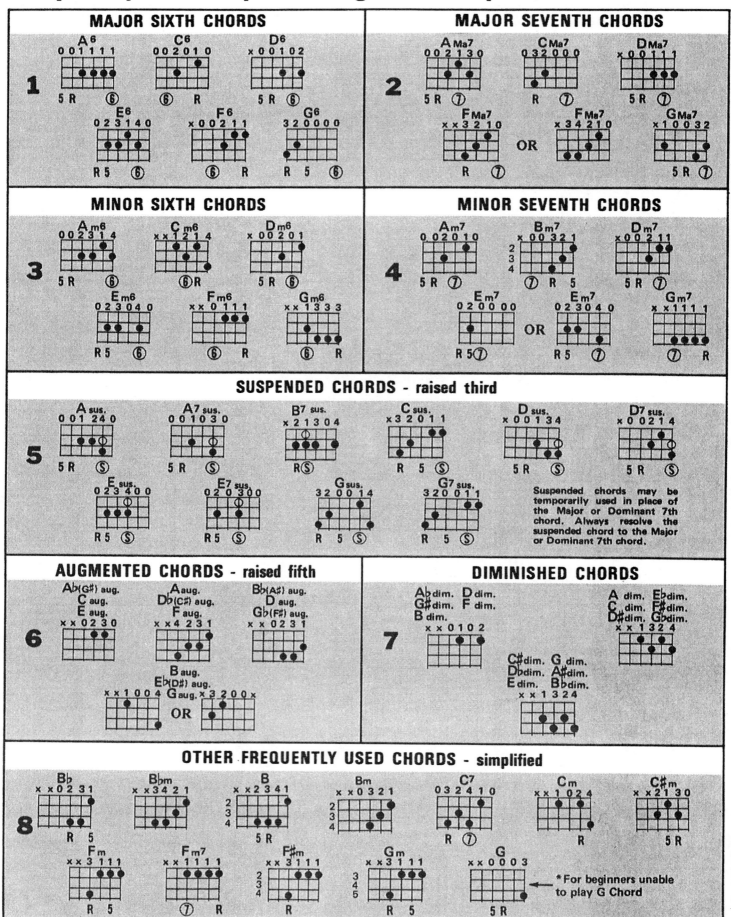

Bar Chords

BAR CHORDS are MOVABLE chords that can be played up and down the finger board since they do not have any "open" strings.

Generally, BAR CHORDS are of two types:

1) movable four string chord formations with the index finger depressing more than one string (Small Bar); fig. 1 and fig. 2.

2) movable six string chord formations with the index finger depressing all six strings (Great Bar). fig. 3 and fig. 4

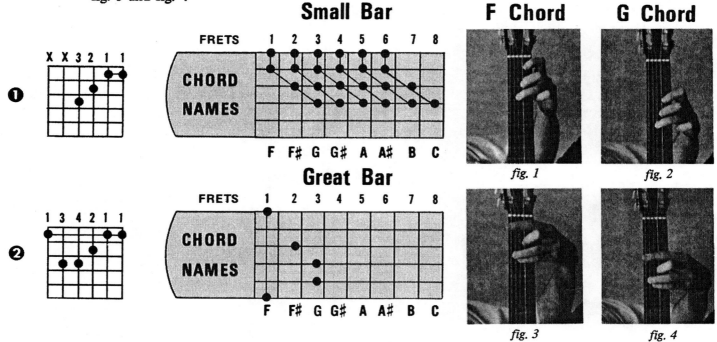

Small Bar

Great Bar

F Chord

fig. 1

G Chord

fig. 2

fig. 3

fig. 4

Bar Technique

To develop the BAR (Great Bar) technique do the following:

1. Place the index finger on the guitar at the THIRD FRET. fig. 5.

2. The INDEX FINGER should be rigid (not bent) from the tip to the knuckle. fig. 5.

3. The THUMB is placed opposite the index finger on the neck under the finger board.

4. WRIST is out.

5. Do not allow the PALM to touch the neck of the guitar.

6. Be sure to apply enough FINGER PRESSURE to eliminate string "buzz".

7. Using the sweep or brush strum, check to see that all strings are sounding.

fig. 5

Do the following exercise on the third or any fret:

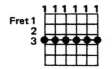

NOTE: Being able to play the Small Bar chord formations does little toward developing the technique required to play the Great Bar chord formations. The authors recommend STARTING with the GREAT BAR — FORM ONE. (see pages 10 and 11)

Bar Chords
CHORD FORMS

Three basic patterns found in the OPEN CHORD formations can be transferred to MOVABLE BAR CHORDS. The authors choose to call these chord patterns: FORM ONE; FORM TWO; and FORM THREE.

FORM ONE

FORM ONE is related to the OPEN E chord positions--E, E7, Em, and Em7. When BARRED, these open string chords become movable Major, Dominant 7th, minor and minor 7th chord positions. They are more difficult than the open string chords because of the BAR technique required of the index finger and the use of the fourth finger.

	MAJOR	MINOR	DOMINANT 7th	MINOR 7th
OPEN E	E	Em	E7	Em7
BAR F	F	Fm	F7	Fm7
BAR F# (G♭)	F#	F#m	F#7	F#m7
BAR G	G	Gm	G7	Gm7

Form One

RELATED TO THE OPEN E FORMS

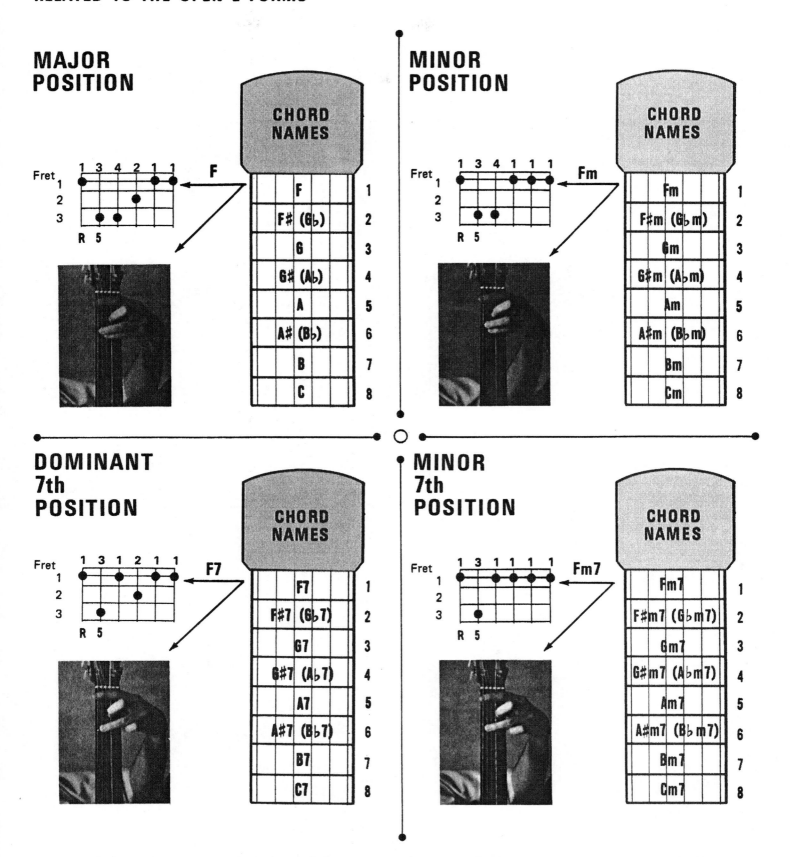

MAJOR POSITION

CHORD NAMES	
F	1
F♯ (G♭)	2
G	3
G♯ (A♭)	4
A	5
A♯ (B♭)	6
B	7
C	8

MINOR POSITION

CHORD NAMES	
Fm	1
F♯m (G♭m)	2
Gm	3
G♯m (A♭m)	4
Am	5
A♯m (B♭m)	6
Bm	7
Cm	8

DOMINANT 7th POSITION

CHORD NAMES	
F7	1
F♯7 (G♭7)	2
G7	3
G♯7 (A♭7)	4
A7	5
A♯7 (B♭7)	6
B7	7
C7	8

MINOR 7th POSITION

CHORD NAMES	
Fm7	1
F♯m7 (G♭m7)	2
Gm7	3
G♯m7 (A♭m7)	4
Am7	5
A♯m7 (B♭m7)	6
Bm7	7
Cm7	8

♪ The NAME of the CHORD is determined by FRET LOCATION of the 1st finger. For example, an A major, would be played at the fifth fret.

Form Two

RELATED TO OPEN C POSITIONS

FORM TWO is related to the open C chord positions—C, C Major 7, C7 and Cm chord. The MOVABLE DOMINANT 7th, FORM TWO, is the most valuable chord for the first year student. Remember fret location and thus the name of the chord is determined by the first finger. See the following examples:

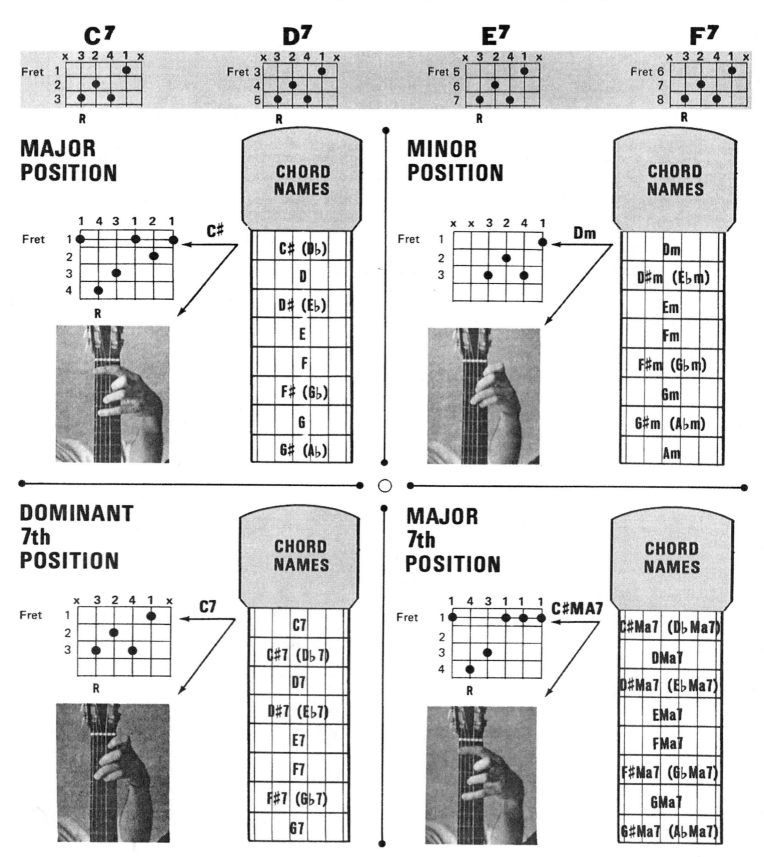

Form Three

RELATED TO THE OPEN A POSITIONS

FORM THREE is related to the open A chord positions–A, A7, A Major7, Am, and Am7. When barred, these chords become movable. The first year student should concentrate on the MOVABLE Minor (Am) and Minor 7th (Am7) chords in Form Three.

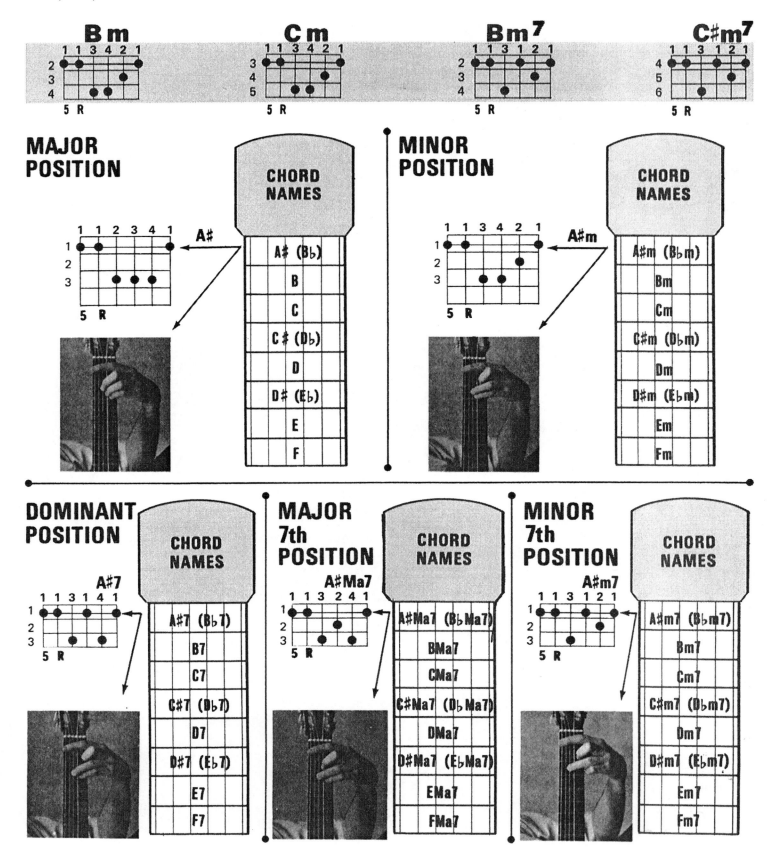

Turn-around

The "turn-around" is often used at the end of a song in preparation for repeating the song. It is sometimes used as an introduction to the song. Practice the following chord progressions giving each chord four Beats:

KEY of C: C - Am - Dm - G7   KEY of G: G - Em - Am - D7   KEY of D: D – Bm – Em – A7

Circle of 5ths

The circle of 5ths is a progression of chords in which the relationship, that is the interval distance between the chords, is a fifth counting backward or a fourth counting forward. It is the *Dominant* (V chord) to the *Tonic* (I chord) relationship that comprises the circle of 5ths.

Next to the I, IV, V chords, the circle of 5ths is probably the most frequently used chord progression in music. The circle may use major, minor and dominant 7th chords in any variety of combinations. Memorize the circle for an aid in learning how to play "by ear". Practice the following chord progressions.

The Circle using Dominant 7th chords:
   B7 – E7 – A7 – D7 – G7 – C7 – F
The Circle using minor chords:
   Bm – Em – Am – Dm – Gm – C7 – F
The Circle using a combination:
   Bm – E7 – Am – D7 – Gm – C7 – F

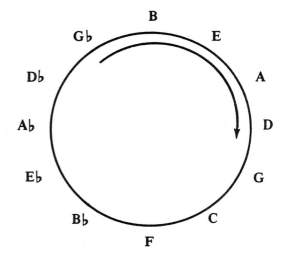

Transposing

It is frequently necessary to transpose a song - that is, change it from one Key to another. An uncomfortable vocal range or the all too frequent use of difficult bar chords might be reasons to transpose the song.

First determine the interval distance between the original key and the new key; that is the number of musical alphabet (ABCDEFG) letters between the two keys. Change each chord the same distance while observing the key signature (♯'s & ♭'s). The following chart will serve as a guide.

Chords
built on scale

Scale

I do	ii re	iii mi	IV fa	V7 sol	vi la	vii° ti	I do
C	Dm	Em	F	G7	Am	B°	C
D	Em	F♯m	G	A7	Bm	C♯°	D
E	F♯m	G♯m	A	B7	C♯m	D♯°	E
G	Am	Bm	C	D7	Em	F♯°	G
A	Bm	C♯m	D	E7	F♯m	G♯°	A
Tonic (Key)			Sub- Dominant	Dominant Seventh	Relative Minor		

Capo

A CAPO may be used to transpose songs to difficult keys while retaining the use of the Basic Open String Chords. For example, it is possible to play in the Key of E♭ by placing the CAPO on the 1ST fret and fingering the D chord at the 3RD fret.

Guitar Strums

You will find that the right hand technique offers perhaps the greatest challenge and is one of the more difficult aspects of the course. This area must be approached gradually and fundamentals of technique must be stressed to prevent potential problems and bad habits.

The major difficulty will most likely be in coordinating the left hand chord patterns with the right hand technique in conjunction with reading the music and singing. The mechanical tasks, therefore, must be drilled (slowly at first until they can be executed without conscious effort). You have mastered the strum when you can carry on a conversation while performing the strum correctly.

A record demonstrating all strums as they appear in this book is available with the Teacher's Manual.

♪NOTE: It is important to understand the difference between "Folk Strums" and "Finger Strums", as described in this section. The "Folk Strums" should be developed before attempting the more difficult "Finger Strums".

Folk Strums

There are a variety of folk strums. Only what may be considered the basic strums are included here. In the beginning use one basic strum for each song — keep it simple. Left hand technique (ability to play chords and chord progressions) must be developed first. As finger dexterity develops and the strums become "grooved", try more variety. The goal is to create original strums and to apply them to songs in an individual manner. Strums are suggested for each song in the Song Section of this book.

RIGHT HAND POSITION

It is the author's intention to use the general elements of the right hand classical guitar position for beginning folk strums. This will lead to a smooth transition from the folk strums to the more difficult finger strums and classical guitar techniques. fig. 1

ARM POSITION

Rest the forearm on the edge of the guitar just above the saddle. The exact position will vary according to the length of fingers, wrist and forearm. fig. 1

THUMB POSITION

The thumb is rigid (not bent) and is placed slightly over the soundhole (mouth) of the guitar. Allow the thumb to hang downward in a normal position above the 4th string. When executing any strum, the thumb must move to the outside of the fingers. fig. 2

FINGER POSITION

The index, middle, and ring fingers should be slightly curved and placed over the rosette above the 1st, 2nd, and 3rd strings. The *hand* should be tilted to the left.

fig. 2

♪ NOTE: The motion of strumming should come from the WRIST and not the arm.

Folk Strums

STRUM SYMBOLS and EXPLANATIONS

SYMBOL	REPRESENTS	TECHNIQUE
T	THUMB	Thumb plucks a single string — generally the root or the 5th of the chord located on the 4th, 5th, or 6th string (rest stroke)*.
S	SWEEP with thumb downward	Thumb strums (sweeps) down across all the strings (low to high).
B	BRUSH with 1st and 2nd fingers downward	Strum (brush) with the backs of the index and middle fingers (nails) down across the strings (low to high).
I	1st FINGER downward	Strum with the back of the 1st finger (nail) down across the strings (low to high).
I	1st FINGER upward	Strum with the fleshy part of the 1st finger upward across the 1st, 2nd, & 3rd strings (high to low).
MUTE	DAMPEN STRINGS	Brush the strings downward with the index or index and middle fingers and then immediately dampen (silence, deaden) with the heel or palm of the hand. Use a continuous motion.
LIFT	LIFT the fingers of the Left hand	Fingers of the left hand are lifted off the fingerboard (from whatever chord is being played) to allow the open strings to sound.

*see explanation on page 20

♪ NOTE: The dot (·) and dash (-) placed over the notes in the strums represent an effort to give the beginning music reader an additional clue as to the relative length of the notes in the strum.

Folk Strums

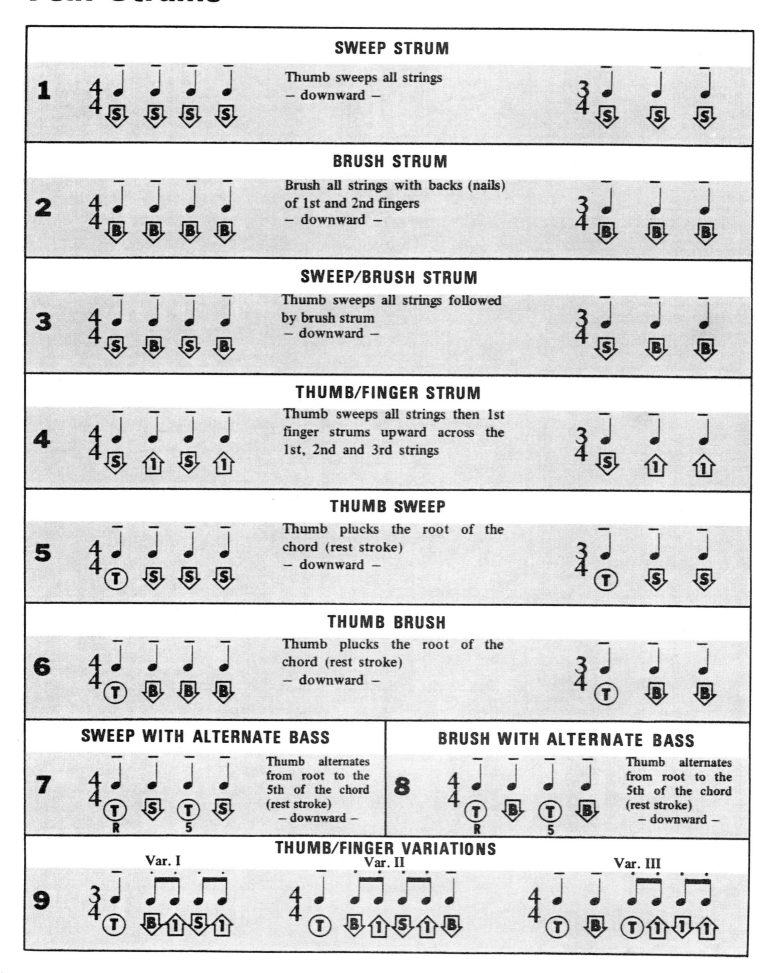

Folk Strums

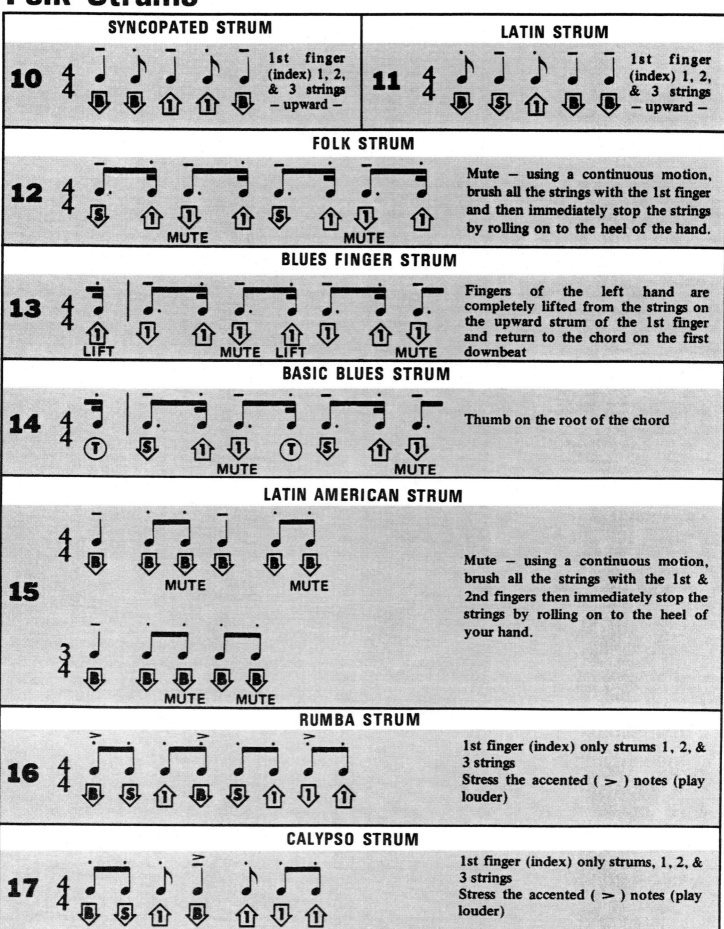

Finger Strums

Finger strums are those strums in which the strings are:

1. plucked simultaneously (together-CHORD).
2. plucked successively (one after another-ARPEGGIO).
3. plucked in a COMBINATION of 1. and 2.

There are a variety of possibilities. The basic finger strums are included here along with an explanation of the necessary right hand technique.

Right Hand Position

The classical guitar position is recommended. This basic right hand position is readily adaptable to playing with a plectrum (pick).

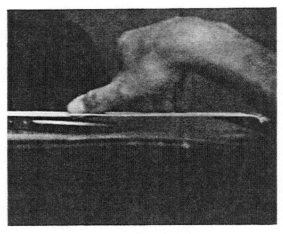

fig. 1

ARM POSITION

Rest the forearm on the edge of the guitar just above the saddle.

THUMB

The thumb is rigid (straight) and is placed just past the beginning of the mouth (soundhole) of the guitar, fig. 1. The thumb may rest on the 5th or 4th strings or hang normally, fig. 2. The thumb will generally play the notes on the 4th, 5th, and 6th strings employing either the rest or free stroke (explanation to follow).

fig. 2

FINGERS

Place the fingers on their tips close to the nails on the following strings:

1. 1st finger on the 3rd or G string.
2. 2nd finger on the 2nd or B string.
3. 3rd finger on the 1st or E string. See fig. 3.

Instead of plucking hard, stroke (free stroke) the strings. The hand should be tilted slightly to the left and does not lift from the guitar. (Use finger motion instead of arm motion).

fig. 3

E.L. 2287

Rest Stroke

Two basic strokes are used in performing strums and notation: 1) the *Rest Stroke*; 2) and the *Free Stroke*.

The *rest stroke* is developed first.

THUMB

Pluck the string downward, fig. 1, and allow the thumb to come to rest on the next (higher in pitch) string, fig. 2 The thumb is rigid (not bent) and moves mainly from the joint at the wrist. Generally use the rest stroke with the thumb as follows:

1. for folk strums
2. to emphasize the bass notes.

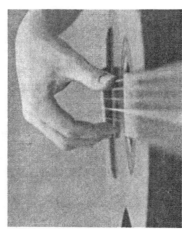

fig. 1

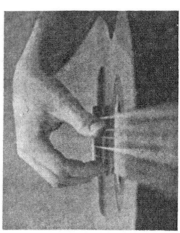

fig. 2

FINGERS

*Keeping the hand steady, press the finger across the string, fig. 3, and come to rest against the next (lower in pitch) string, fig. 4. The resulting tone is produced by a combination of the fleshy part of the finger followed immediately by the striking of the nail. The index finger and middle finger are to alternate on successive single notes, fig. 5 and fig. 6. Use the rest stroke with the fingers as follows:

1. for playing single notes
   (as in a melody)
2. to emphasize certain notes.

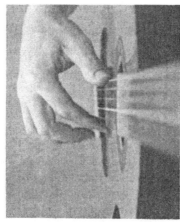

fig. 3

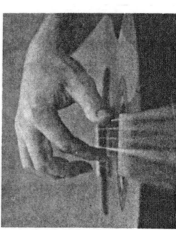

fig. 4

fig. 5

fig. 6

NOTE: *HAND POSITION* — The hand should be tilted slightly more to the left when playing the *rest stroke* with the fingers. It is suggsted that the *rest stroke* (finger) be learned by rote so it may be applied to the beginning notation exercises. Alternate the index and middle fingers. (see page 30).

Free Stroke

In the free stroke the thumb and fingers do not come to rest on adjacent strings; they pass over the adjacent strings.

THUMB

The thumb (rigid—not bent), fig. 1, moves over the adjacent string and to the outside of the index finger, fig. 2. The thumb motion is to be independent of the hand. Hold the hand steady. Use the free stroke with the thumb as follows:

1. for the pull, and pinch strums
2. for arpeggios.
3. for chords.

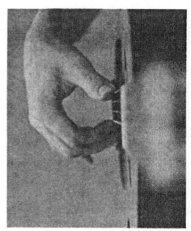
fig. 1

fig. 2

FINGERS

The fingers are slightly more curved than in the rest stroke, fig. 3 & 5. The fingers pass over the adjacent (lower in pitch) strings, fig. 4 & 6. The stroke is to be executed with independent "finger action". Do not move the hand or pull with the arm. Generally, the 1st, 2nd, and 3rd fingers are placed on the 3rd, 2nd, and 1st strings respectively. Use the fingers in the free stroke as follows:

1. for finger strums
   (arpeggio, pinch, pull)
2. for single note passages which do not need to be emphasized.

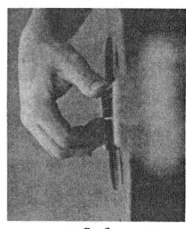
fig. 3

fig. 4

fig. 5

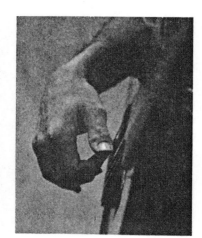
fig. 6

♪ NOTE: A better tone quality will be produced if the *nails* of the right hand are properly shaped and cared for. The nails should be shaped to the contour of the fleshy part of the finger. They should not extend further than 1/16 of an inch beyond the end of the finger.

Finger Strums
SYMBOLS and EXPLANATIONS

SYMBOL	REPRESENTS	TECHNIQUE
1	1st FINGER	Index finger plucks the 3rd string. Note: Exceptions are usually clearly indicated. (free stroke)*
2	2nd FINGER	Middle finger plucks the 2nd string. (free stroke)
3	3rd FINGER	Ring finger plucks the first string. (free stroke)
3 2	3rd & 2nd FINGERS	Ring finger (1st string) and middle finger (2nd string) pluck together.
3 2 1	3rd, 2nd & 1st FINGERS	Ring, middle, and index fingers pluck the 3rd, 2nd, & 1st strings together (all at the same time).
3 2 1 T	PULL STRUM	Fingers and thumb (thumb plucks the root or 5th of the chord) are plucked together.
3/T 2/T 1/T	PINCH STRUM	3rd, 2nd, or 1st fingers are plucked (pinch) with the thumb (thumb plucks the root or 5th of the chord).

♪ NOTE: *An explanation of the free and rest stroke and their application can be found on the preceding pages.

Finger Strums

ARPEGGIO STRUM NO. 1

1 3/4 (T) 1 2 3 2 1

Thumb on the root of the chord. 1, 2, & 3, fingers pluck separately (free stroke)

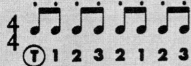 4/4 (T) 1 2 3 2 1 2 3

ARPEGGIO STRUM NO. 2

2 3/4 (T) 1 2 1 3 1

Thumb on the root of the chord or alternate to the 5th when repeating the strum

 4/4 (T) 1 2 1 3 1 2 1

ARPEGGIO STRUM NO. 3

3 3/4 (T) 1 2 (T) 1 2

Thumb on the root of the chord or alternate to the 5th

 4/4 (T) 1 2 3 (T) 1 2 3

CALYPSO STRUM

4 4/4 (T) 1 2 3 2 1 2

Accent (>) the 3rd finger; i.e., stress and play heavier and louder
Thumb on the root of the chord (Rest stroke) Fingers use free stroke

RUMBA NO. 1

5 4/4 (T) 1 2 (T) 1 2 (T) 1
R 5 5

Alternate Thumb from bass to 5th as indicated.

Finger Strums

BASIC PLUCKING STRUM

6 Thumb on the root of the chord (rest stroke) 1, 2 & 3 fingers pluck together (free stroke)

PLUCKING STRUM WITH ALTERNATE BASS

7 Thumb alternates from the root to the 5th of the chord (rest stroke)

Fingers pluck together (free stroke)

PLUCKING STRUM NO. 1

8 2nd and 3rd fingers pluck together (free stroke)

PLUCKING STRUM NO. 2

9 Slightly accent the first and third beats with the thumb (rest stroke)

Alternate to 5th — optional

PLUCKING STRUM NO. 3

10 Emphasize the accented note

Alternate to 5th — optional

Finger Strums

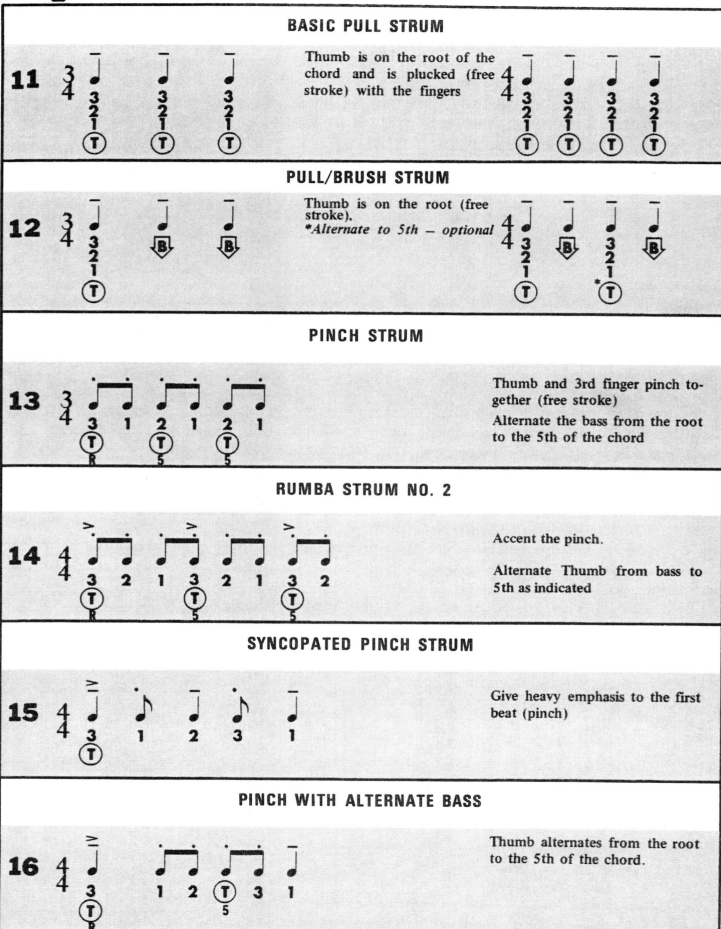

BASIC PULL STRUM

11 — Thumb is on the root of the chord and is plucked (free stroke) with the fingers

PULL/BRUSH STRUM

12 — Thumb is on the root (free stroke).
*Alternate to 5th — optional

PINCH STRUM

13 — Thumb and 3rd finger pinch together (free stroke)
Alternate the bass from the root to the 5th of the chord

RUMBA STRUM NO. 2

14 — Accent the pinch.
Alternate Thumb from bass to 5th as indicated

SYNCOPATED PINCH STRUM

15 — Give heavy emphasis to the first beat (pinch)

PINCH WITH ALTERNATE BASS

16 — Thumb alternates from the root to the 5th of the chord.

Finger-Picking Strums

Finger-picking strums have TWO distinguishing characteristics: 1) Thumb pattern; 2) Finger position.

THUMB PATTERN

The Thumb (T) plays on EVERY DOWN BEAT alternating between the root of the chord, and the THIRD STRING. In ⁴⁄₄, the Thumb will pluck the Root of the chord on the 1st and 3rd beats and will alternate to the THIRD STRING on the 2nd and 4th beats.

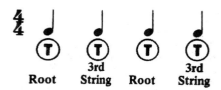

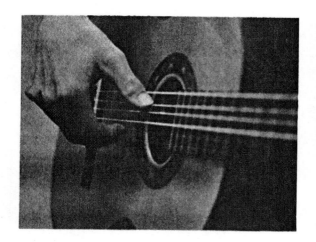

FINGER POSITION

Place the fingers as follows:
1. 1st finger on the second or B string.
2. 2nd finger on the first or E string, fig. 1 & 2.

♪ NOTE: The 3rd finger will not be used.

fig. 2

To develop the Finger-Picking technique, practice the following sequence using a G chord:

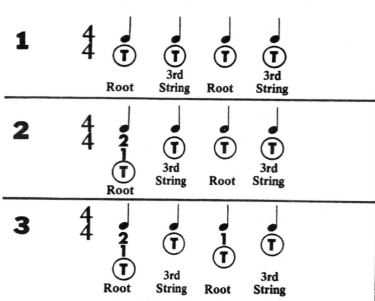

Exercises 1, 2 and 3 should prepare you for the following Finger-Picking Strums. Maintain the same alternating pattern.

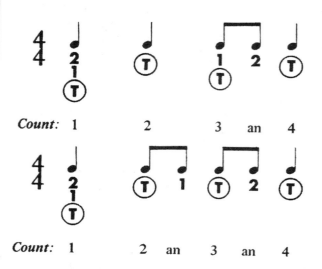

♪ NOTE: This is only an introduction to the Finger-Picking style. There are many variations and possibilities.

Flat-Pick Technique

HOW TO HOLD THE PICK

The flat-pick (plectrum) is held between THUMB and the SIDE of the INDEX FINGER. Follow these steps.

1. Place the THUMB (from the tip to the first joint) on the side of the INDEX FINGER. (fig. 1)

2. The THUMB should be PARALLEL to the INDEX FINGER and should extend just past the first joint. (fig. 2)

3. Insert roughly half of the pick between the THUMB and INDEX FINGER so as to allow a triangle shape to be exposed. (This will vary with the size of the pick). (fig. 2)

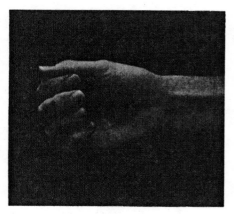

fig. 1

DOWN STROKE

The down stroke is played two ways:

1. REST STROKE — pick comes to rest on the next string. Use this method when you want emphasis.

2. FREE STROKE — pick does not come to rest on the adjacent string. Use this method in rapid passages that require alternating between the down and up strokes.

STRUM SYMBOLS AND EXPLANATIONS

fig. 2

SYMBOL	REPRESENTS	TECHNIQUE
/	HASH MARK Quarter Note	Strum (sweep) down across all the strings (low to high) as in playing chords. Represents one beat.
⊓	DOWN STROKE	Strike a single string with a downward motion as in playing melody. (See above description of down stroke)
V	UP STROKE	Strike a single string with an upward motion. Generally the upstroke is used for notes played on the up beat

Music Signs And Symbols

The STAFF consists of 5 LINES and 4 SPACES. Notes placed on the staff designate a DEFINITE PITCH. LEGER LINES are for EXTENDING the staff above or below. The CLEF sign placed on the staff establishes the names of the notes. Guitar notation uses the TREBLE or G CLEF. The first SEVEN LETTERS of the ALPHABET are used to NAME THE NOTES — A B︿C D E︿F G (︿ = ½ step)

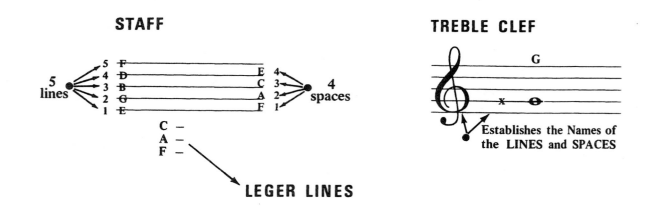

STAFF   **TREBLE CLEF**

Establishes the Names of the LINES and SPACES

LEGER LINES

NOTES ON THE STAFF

The staff is divided by BAR LINES. The space between one bar line and the next is called a MEASURE.

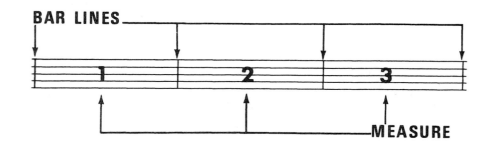

BAR LINES

1   2   3

MEASURE

Each measure contains a specific number of beats as established by the TIME SIGNATURE. The TOP NUMBER of the time signature tells how many BEATS are in each measure. The BOTTOM NUMBER of the time signature tells what kind of NOTE receives ONE BEAT.

2/4 — Two beats in each measure — Quarter note gets one beat

3/4 — Three beats in each measure — Quarter note gets one beat

4/4 — Four beats in each measure — Quarter note gets one beat

Note Values and Rests

To understand the values of NOTES and RESTS (signs of silence) in music, you must understand what is meant by BEAT. The beat is the regularly or sometimes irregularly recurring pulsation of the music. When listening to music, tap your foot to the beat of the music. You will discover that the BEAT is divided into:

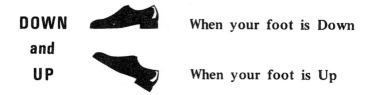

DOWN   When your foot is Down

and

UP   When your foot is Up

Rhythm Chart

The following charts indicate HOW MANY BEATS various NOTES and RESTS would get in ♩ time. You can accurately measure the duration of each note by: (1) TAPPING your FOOT — to keep track of the beat, (2) by COUNTING the number of beats given to each note. Notice that in the case of the EIGHTH NOTE a note is played on both the DOWN and UP of the BEAT.

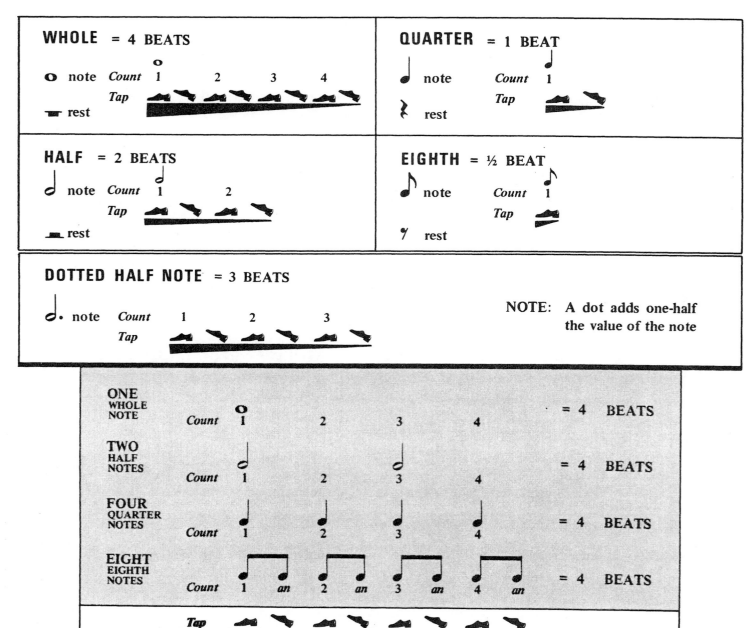

Guitar Notation Symbols

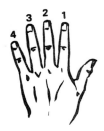

LEFT HAND

0 = Open strings
1 = 1st finger
2 = 2nd finger
3 = 3rd finger
4 = 4th finger

NUMBERS placed next to the NOTES tell which FINGER of the LEFT HAND to use. CIRCLED NUMBERS —
⑥ ⑤ ④ ③ ② ① — are used to point out WHICH STRING to pluck.

RIGHT HAND

p = thumb (pulgar)
i = index (indice)
m = middle (medio)
a = ring (anular)

OPEN STRINGS

p, i, m, a — placed above or below the notes tell WHICH FINGERS of the RIGHT HAND to use.

Preparation for Reading Music

The following ROTE EXERCISES should be mastered before proceding to the notation exercises in order to develop a SENSATION of POSITION and MOVEMENT of the HANDS. (KINESTHETIC FEELING)

RIGHT HAND

Exercise 1 is for the RIGHT HAND. While plucking OPEN STRINGS the Right Hand will practice the REST STROKE with the FINGERS (index and middle). ALTERNATE the fingers. A thorough description of the REST STROKE technique may be found in the Strum Section. This exercise will be limited to the 1st, 2nd and 3rd open strings (E, B and G). Practice backwards also.

LEFT HAND

Exercise 2 is for the LEFT HAND in combination with the RIGHT HAND. DO NOT RAISE THE FINGERS OF THE LEFT HAND UNTIL NECESSARY. For example, leave the 1st finger in place on the fingerboard while the 2nd finger is fingering the desired note.

♪ NOTE: Also practice Ex. 2 playing each note once or twice. Play the exercise backwards as well.

E.L. 2287

Open Strings

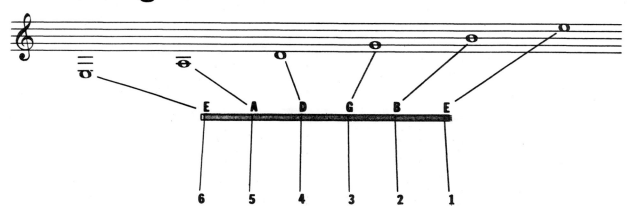

OPEN E STRING (1st STRING)

Repeat Sign

OPEN B STRING (2nd STRING)

OPEN G STRING (3rd STRING)

♪ NOTE: Exercises 3, 4, and 5 may be played together as a trio.

Review: Open Treble Strings

♪ NOTE: *G, Em, and C indicate chord accompaniment that may be added to the exercise.

OPEN D STRING (4th STRING)

Use the REST STROKE with the Thumb (*p*) for the following exercises

OPEN A STRING (5th STRING)

OPEN E STRING (6th STRING)

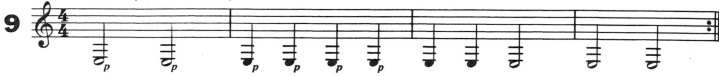

E.L. 2287

Review: Open Bass Strings

♦ ◇ **REVIEW:** Review of the OPEN STRINGS with chord accompaniment. Be sure to use the REST STROKE with the THUMB (p) and the FINGERS. ALTERNATE index (i) and middle (m) fingers.

Notes on the 1st String

♪ ***NOTE:** Leave the 1st finger down while playing the G with the 3rd finger. The general rule is to leave the fingers of the left hand down until they have to be lifted.

Notes on the 2nd String

♪ **NOTE:** Exercises 15 and 16 may be played together. Add chord accompaniment.

Review: Notes on the 1st and 2nd Strings

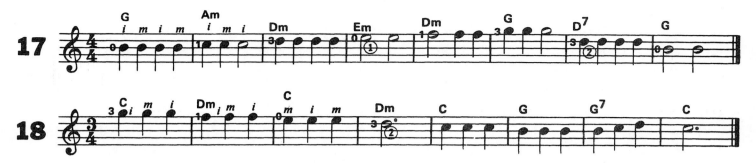

Exercise 19 is a DUET for two guitars or the teacher may divide the class. Play guitar parts I and II together. Add the chord accompaniment. Try a variety of strums.

Notes on the 3rd String

Au Clair de lune

Review: Notes on the 1st, 2nd and 3rd Strings

GUITAR TRIO   Three separate parts - I, II, and III - may be performed together with an added chord accompaniment.

Review: Open 4th, 5th and 6th

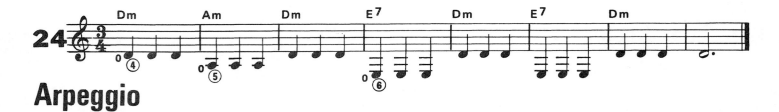

Arpeggio

An ARPEGGIO is a "broken chord" pattern in which the notes of the chord are played ONE AFTER THE OTHER. Correct technique is difficult and must be practiced carefully. Use the FREE STROKE. Correct hand position is explained in the strum section on page 21.

New Note - G Sharp

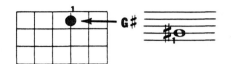

SHARP (♯) RAISES the pitch a half step — up one fret on the guitar

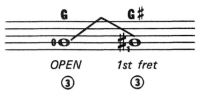

> *NOTE: Play the G sharp for the entire measure. The sharp sign need only to be indicated once for each measure.

Arpeggio Studies

Use the same RIGHT HAND techniques developed in playing the FINGER STRUM ARPEGGIOS. Refer to the STRUM SECTION for further explanation of the REST STROKE and FREE STROKE. To facilitate the following studies, the LEFT HAND may finger the chords indicated — or observe the fingering indicated next to each note. Place the fingers in position before playing the arpeggio. The sign ⅞ means repeat the previous measure.

STUDY 1

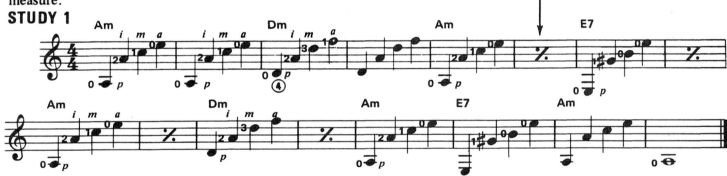

> NOTE: Keep the fingers of the LEFT HAND in position on the fingerboard until they have to be moved. Also, the BASS NOTES — D, A, and E - should be allowed to ring through each measure.

STUDY 2
STUDY 3
STUDY 4

ARPEGGIO AND REST STROKE

Study 5 requires the FINGERS of the RIGHT HAND to change from playing single note melody (REST STROKE) to the arpeggio technique (FREE STROKE). Practice the Study slowly working for smoothness and control. The HAND should be tilted slightly more to the left when playing the REST STROKE with the fingers.

STUDY 5

EIGHTH NOTES

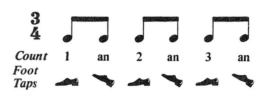

OPEN STRINGS

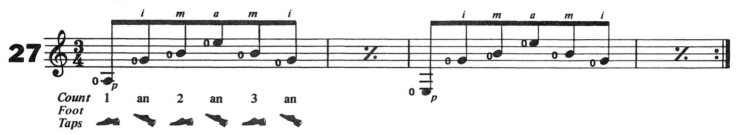

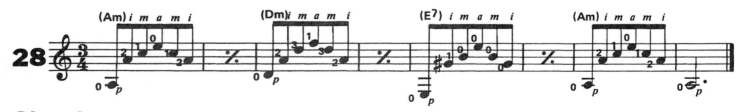

Chords

Two or more tones sounded simultaneously result in a CHORD. The guitar technique used to play CHORDS is the same as was used to play the PULL and PINCH STRUMS. Refer to the STRUM section for more detailed information concerning HAND POSITION and the FREE STROKE technique.

OPEN STRINGS

Chords in Am

The FINGERS of the LEFT HAND should be placed on the notes forming the chord before plucking the strings with the right hand. Use the FREE STROKE.

CHORDS AND ARPEGGIO STUDIES

Generally use the FREE STROKE. For emphasis of the bass notes, the thumb may use the rest stroke when practical.

STUDY 6

STUDY 7

CHORDS may also be played by pulling or pinching the fingers and the thumb together at the same time. This technique is similar to that used in the Pull and Pinch Strums. In the following exercises, use the FREE STROKE. Be careful that the THUMB moves to the outside of the INDEX FINGER.

Am Studies

There are many signs and symbols used in music notation. D. C. (Da Capo) al fine means to go back to the beginning and play to the end (fine).

STUDY 8

Music may be made more EXPRESSIVE if contrasts between loud and soft are made. DYNAMIC SIGNS refer to the degree of loudness or softness of a tone.

DYNAMIC SIGNS			
pp	Pianissimo	Very soft	
p	Piano	Soft	
mp	Mezzo Piano	Moderately soft	
mf	Mezzo Forte	Moderately loud	
f	Forte	Loud	
ff	Fortissimo	Very loud	

Cresc. – Crescendo	Gradually louder
Dim. – Diminuendo	Gradually softer
Decresc. – Decrescendo	Gradually softer
Morendo	Dying away
——————	Gradually louder
——————	Gradually softer

STUDY 9

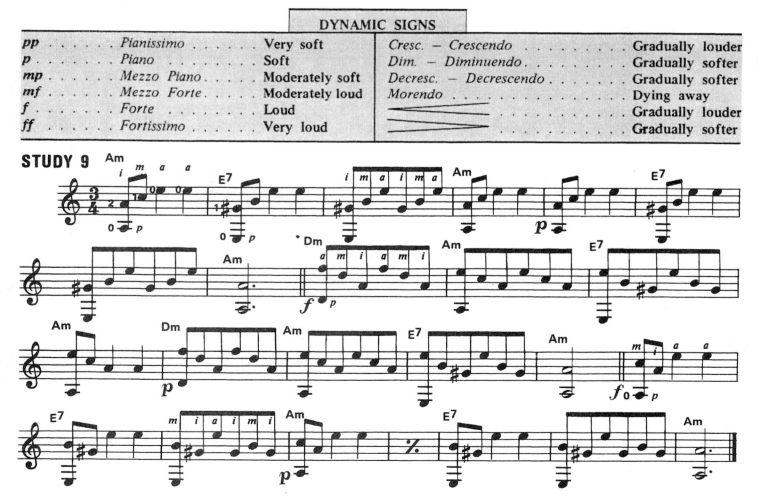

Notes on the 4th String

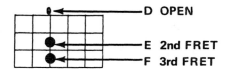

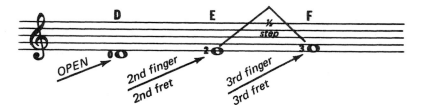

Notes on the 5th String

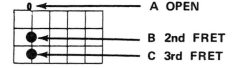

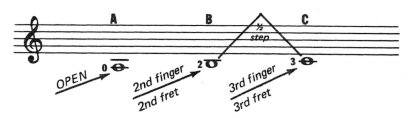

Notes on the 6th String

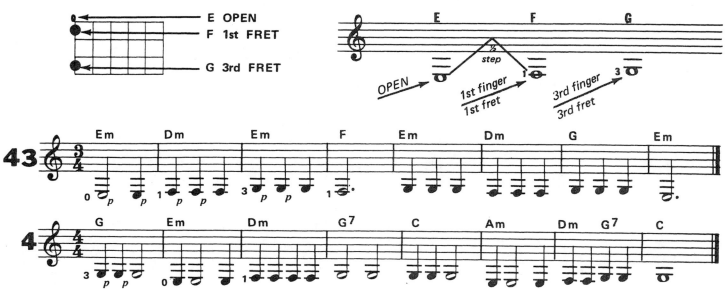

First Position

The location of the INDEX FINGER of the LEFT HAND on the FRET of the guitar determines the NAME of the POSITION. In FIRST POSITION, the INDEX FINGER of the left hand is located on the FIRST FRET.

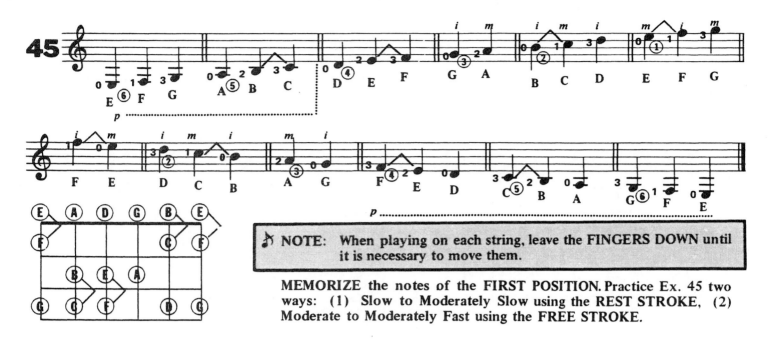

NOTE: When playing on each string, leave the FINGERS DOWN until it is necessary to move them.

MEMORIZE the notes of the FIRST POSITION. Practice Ex. 45 two ways: (1) Slow to Moderately Slow using the REST STROKE, (2) Moderate to Moderately Fast using the FREE STROKE.

CHORDS AND ARPEGGIOS IN C

Music Theory

INTERVALS

The DIFFERENCE in PITCH between two tones is called the INTERVAL. The smallest interval is the HALF STEP. The distance from fret to fret on the guitar fingerboard is a half step. A WHOLE STEP would be the distance between the 1st and 3rd fret.

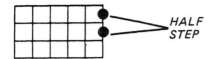

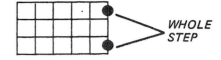

SCALES

SCALES are a certain arrangement of successive tones according to their interval distance from each other. Scales provide the skeleton upon which the melody and harmony of songs are based.

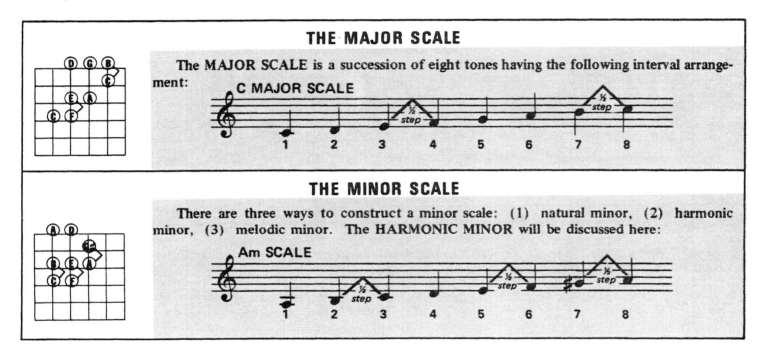

THE MAJOR SCALE

The MAJOR SCALE is a succession of eight tones having the following interval arrangement:

C MAJOR SCALE

THE MINOR SCALE

There are three ways to construct a minor scale: (1) natural minor, (2) harmonic minor, (3) melodic minor. The HARMONIC MINOR will be discussed here:

Am SCALE

CHORDS

The simultaneous sounding of several tones, usually two or more is a CHORD. TRIADS, chords of three tones, are the most frequently used in guitar playing . Triads consist of a ROOT, THIRD, and FIFTH above the root. The triad is the basis for our harmony system and is related to the scales — Major and minor. The most important triads are those built upon the I, IV and V degrees of the scale.

C MAJOR SCALE

A MINOR SCALE

KEY SIGNATURES

A song based on the C MAJOR SCALE is in the KEY OF C. The I (C), IV (F), and V (G) chords will provide the basic harmonic structure. A song based on the A MINOR SCALE is in the KEY OF A MINOR. The principle chords would be the I (Am), IV (Dm), and V (E).

E.L. 2287

CAPRICE NO. 1

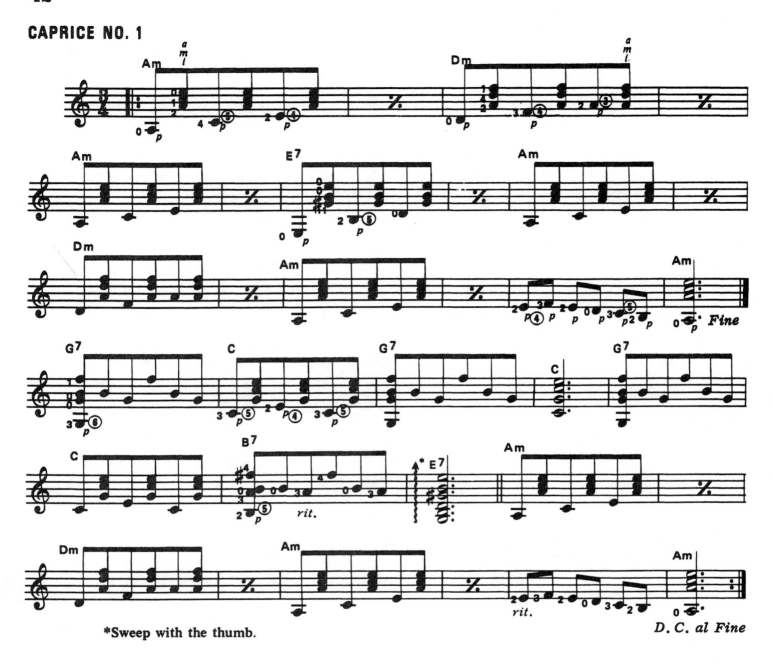

*Sweep with the thumb.

D. C. al Fine

CARULLI STUDY

This Little Light Of Mine

FOLK STRUM NO. 10 SYNCOPATED STRUM

Hava Nagila

BRUSH WITH ALTERNATE BASS

FOLK STRUM NO. 8

Down In The Valley

SWEEP OR BRUSH STRUM
FOLK STRUM NO. 1 or NO. 2

1. Down in the Val - ley Val - ley so low. _____
2. Build me a cas - tle for - ty feet high _____
3. Write me a let - ter send it by mail _____

Hang your head o ver hear the wind blow. _____
so I can see him as he rides by. _____
send it in care of Bir - ming - ham jail. _____

He's Got The Whole World In His Hands

SWEEP/BRUSH
STRUM NO. 3

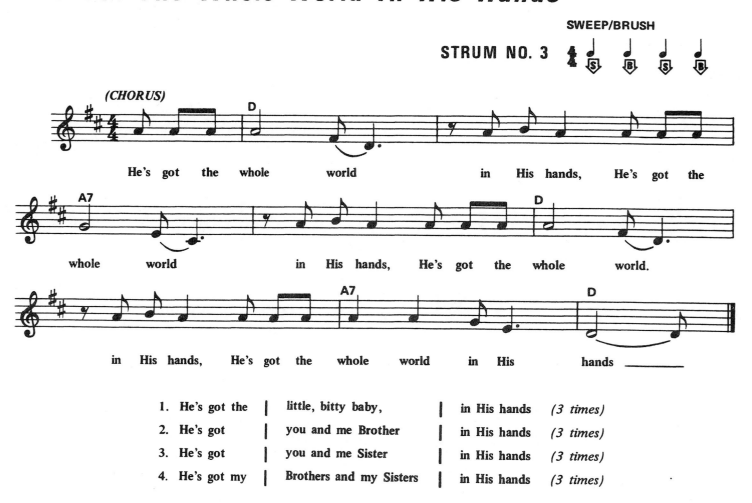

(CHORUS)

He's got the whole world in His hands, He's got the

whole world in His hands, He's got the whole world.

in His hands, He's got the whole world in His hands _____

1. He's got the | little, bitty baby, | in His hands *(3 times)*
2. He's got | you and me Brother | in His hands *(3 times)*
3. He's got | you and me Sister | in His hands *(3 times)*
4. He's got my | Brothers and my Sisters | in His hands *(3 times)*

Good News

FOLK STRUM NO. 3

SWEEP/BRUSH

(CHORUS)

Good News, char-i-ots com-in', Good News, char-i-ots com-in', Good

News, char-i-ots com-in' and I don't want it to leave a-me be-hind.

(VERSE)

There'll be peace and free-dom in this world, I know. There'll be peace and free-dom in this world, I know. There'll be

peace and free-dom in this world I know. And I don't want it to leave a-me be-hind.

(TO CHORUS)

2. There's a | long white robe in the | heavens, I know. *(3 times)*
3. There's a | pair of wings in the | heavens, I know. *(3 times)*
4. There's a | starry crown in the | heavens, I know. *(3 times)*

Rocka My Soul

THUMB/BRUSH

FOLK STRUM NO. 6

Rock-a my soul in the bos-om of Ab-ra-ham, Rock-a my soul in the bos-om of Ab-ra-ham,

Rock-a my soul in the bos-om of Ab-ra ham Oh, Rock-a my soul

So high, you can't get ov-er it so low you can't get un-der it

So wide you can't get 'round ____ it Oh Rock-a my soul.

Banks Of The Ohio

BRUSH W/ALTERNATE BASS

FOLK STRUM NO. 8

2. I held a | knife | against her | breast | As into my
3. I started | home | 'tween twelve and | one | I cried, "My

2. arms | she | pressed | she cried, "Oh | Willie | don't murder
3. God | what have I | done" | killed the | on- | ly women I

2. me | I'm not pre - | pared | for eterni- | ty *(Chorus)*
3. loved, | because she | would | not be my | bride.

48
Worried Man Blues

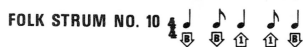

SYNCOPATED STRUM

FOLK STRUM NO. 10

CHORUS I. It takes a wor - ried man to sing a wor - ried song. It takes a wor - ried

man to sing a wor - ried song. It takes a wor - ried man to sing a wor - ried

song. I'm wor - ried now _____ but I won't be wor - ried long. _____

| 2. I | went across the | river and | I lay down to | sleep *(repeat 3 times)* |
| 3. | Twenty-nine | links of chain | around my | leg *(repeat 3 times)* |

		A7			**D**
2.	when I woke	up	had	shackles on my	feet *(To Chorus)*
3.	And on each	link	an i -	nitial of my	name *(To Chorus)*

Tom Dooley

FOLK STRUM NOS. 5, 6, 7 or 8

(CHORUS) *G   D7

Hang down your head Tom Doo - ley   hang down your head and cry.

Hang down your head Tom Doo - ley   poor boy your bound _ to die.

(VERSE)

1. Met her on the moun - tain there I took her life.

(TO CHORUS)

Met her on the moun - tain stabbed her _____ with _ a knife.

	G			**D7**
2. This time to -	mor - row	reckon where I'll	be - -
3. This time to -	mor - row	reckon where I'll	be - -

			G
2. If it weren't for	Grayson I'd	be in Tennes -	see.
3. Down in some lonesome	valley	hangin' from a white oak	tree.

Gotta Travel On

On Top Of Old Smoky

Pay Me My Money Down

1. I thought I heard the cap-tain say. — Pay me my mon-ey down — To-
mor-row is our sail-ing day — Pay me my mon-ey down —

(CHORUS)

Pay me — oh pay me — Pay me my mon-ey down —

Pay me or go to jail — Pay me my mon-ey down. —

		A			**E7**
1.	As	soon as the boat was	clear of the bay,	Pay me my	money down. He
2.	I	wish I was Mr.	Howard's son.	Pay me my	money down.

	A		
1. knocked me down with the	end of spar,	Pay me my	money down.	*(Chorus)*
2. sit in the house and	drink good rum,	Pay me my	money down.	*(Chorus)*

Hold On

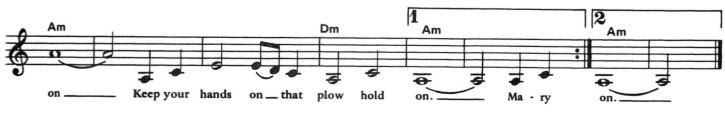

1. No - ah, No - ah, let me come in Doors all fast-ened and the win-dows pinned —
2. wore three links of chain Ev - ery link was Je - sus name —

— Keep your hands on — that plow, hold on. — Hold on — Hold

on — Keep your hands on — that plow hold on. — Ma - ry on.

What Shall We Do With A Drunken Sailor?

VARIATION #3

FOLK STRUM NO. 9

2. | Throw him in the long boat | 'til he's sober | (3 times) | Earlye in the | morning. | (Chorus)
3. | Pull out the plug and | wet him all over | (3 times) | Earlye in the | morning. | (Chorus)
4. | Shave his belly with a | rusty razor | (3 times) | Earlye in the | morning. | (Chorus)
5. | Give him a hair of the | dog that bit him | (3 times) | Earlye in the | morning. | (Chorus)

(Am G   Am columns above: Earlye in the | morning.)

Swing Low Sweet Chariot

FOLK STRUM NO. 12

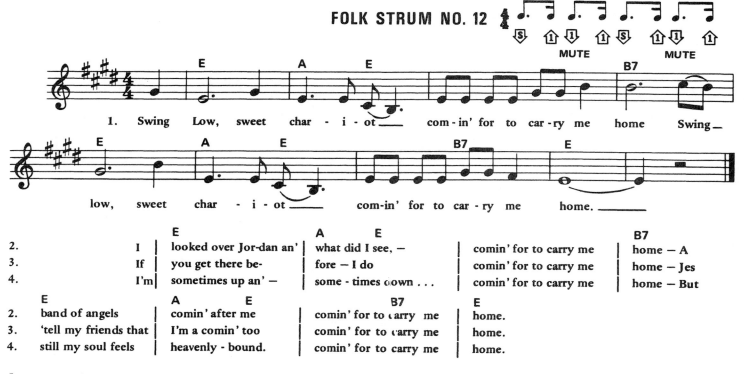

2. | I | looked over Jor-dan an' | what did I see, — | comin' for to carry me | home — A
3. | If | you get there be- | fore — I do | comin' for to carry me | home — Jes
4. | I'm | sometimes up an' — | some - times down . . . | comin' for to carry me | home — But

2. band of angels | comin' after me | comin' for to carry me | home.
3. 'tell my friends that | I'm a comin' too | comin' for to carry me | home.
4. still my soul feels | heavenly - bound. | comin' for to carry me | home.

5. repeat 1st verse.

Blues Progression

#13 BLUES FINGER STRUM
#14 BASIC BLUES STRUM
FOLK STRUM NO. 13 and NO. 14

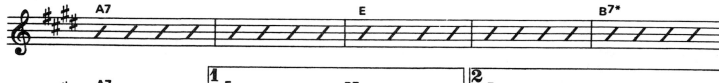

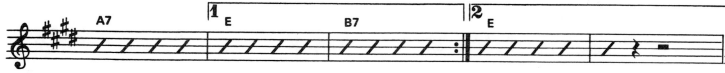

This Train Is Bound For Glory

VARIATION #3

FOLK STRUM NO. 9

1. This train is bound for glor - y, this train _____

This train is bound for glor - y, this train _____

This train is bound for glor - y. Don't ride noth-in' but the

righ-teous and ho - ly, This train is bound for glor - y this train. _____

	E			
2. This train don't	carry no gamblers,	this train	/ / / /
3. This train don't	carry no jokers, well,	this train	/ / / /

		B7	
2. This train don't	carry no gamblers,	this train	/ / / /
3. This train don't	carry no jokers,	this train	/ / / /

	E	E7	A
2. This train don't	carry no gamblers	no crap shooters, no
3 This train don't	carry no jokers, no	high-toned women, no

		B7	E
2. midnight ramblers.	This train don't	carry no gamblers	This train.
3. cigar smokers,	This train don't	carry no jokers, well	This train.

John Henry

FOLK STRUM NO. 12

1. When John Hen - ry was a lit - tle ba - by _____ sit - ting on his dad - dy's

knee "Said the Big Bend Tun - nel on the C and O road gon - na

be the death __ of me, Lord, Lord gon - na be the death __ of me.

2. John | C Henry had a little | woman - And her | name was Mary Magda -
G7 lene - She would | C go to the tunnel and | F sing for John, just to
C hear John Henry's hammer | ring, Lord, Lord, just | hear John Henry's hammer | ring.

Every Night When The Sun Goes Down

FOLK STRUM NO. 11 or NO. 17   LATIN STRUM   CALYPSO STRUM

1. Ev - 'ry night _____ when the sun goes down. _____ Ev - 'ry

night _____ when the sun goes down. _____ Ev - 'ry night _____ when the sun goes

down _____ I hang my head _____ And mourn - ful cry. _____

2. True love, don't | C weep | G7 true love don't | C mourn,
Em True love, don't | weep | C7 true love don't | G7 mourn,
Dm7 True love, don't | weep | G7 true love don't | Am mourn,
Dm7 I'm going a - | way | G7 to marble | C town.

John B. Sails

Delia's Gone

2. Sent for the | doctor - the | doctor came too | late.
Delia, oh | Delia - Where | have you been so | long. The
Send for the | minister to | lay out Delia | straight. *(To Chorus)*
folks they all are | saying, that | you are dead and | gone. *(To Chorus)*

Nobody Knows The Trouble I've Seen

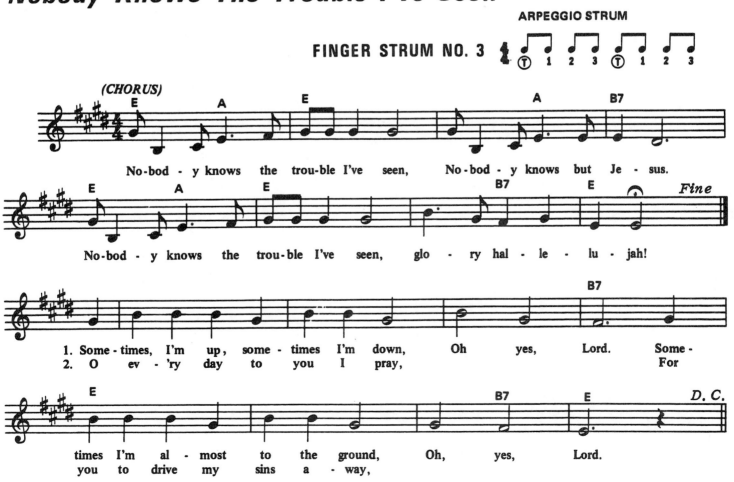

1. Some - times, I'm up, some - times I'm down, Oh yes, Lord. Some -
2. O ev - 'ry day to you I pray, For

times I'm al - most to the ground, Oh, yes, Lord.
you to drive my sins a - way,

Greensleeves

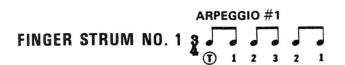

NOTE: The Carol "What Child is This" has the same melody as "Greensleeves."

What Child Is This

	Em		D		C	
1. What	Child is	this, who	laid to	rest on	Mary's	lap is
2.	bring Him	in-cense,	gold and	myrrh, Come	pea-sant	king to

	B7		Em		D		C
1. sleep	ing. Whom	angels	greet with	anthems	sweet, while	shepherds
2. own	Him; The	King of	kings sal -	vation	brings; Let	loving

	B7	Em		G		D	
1. watch are	keep	ing?	This,	this is	Christ	King: Whom
2. hearts en -	throne	Him.	This	this is	Christ	King: Whom

	C		B7		G	
1. shepherds	guard and	angels	sing:	Haste	haste to
2. shepherds	guard	angels	sing:	Haste,	haste to

	D		C	B7	Em	
1. bring Him	laud, The	Babe, the	Son of	Ma -	ry. So
2. bring Him	laud, The	Babe, the	Son of	Ma -	ry.

Johnny Has Gone For A Soldier

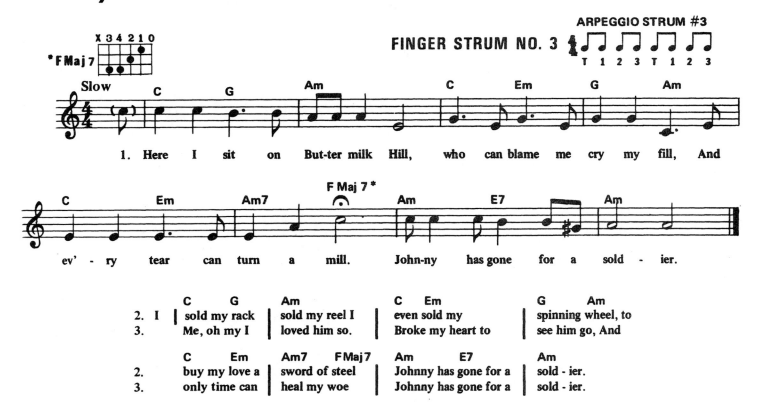

2. I sold my rack | sold my reel I | even sold my | spinning wheel, to
3. Me, oh my I | loved him so. | Broke my heart to | see him go, And

2. buy my love a | sword of steel | Johnny has gone for a | sold - ier.
3. only time can | heal my woe | Johnny has gone for a | sold - ier.

Barbara Allen

2. Twas in the | merry month of | may - the green buds | they were
3. He sent his | ser - vant to the | town to the | place where she was
4. Then slowly | slowly got she | up and slowly | went she
5. "Oh yes I'm | sick, I'm very | sick And never | will be

2. swellin' sweet | Williams on his | death bed lay, for | love of Barbara | Allen.
3. dwelling, Said " | My master bids you | come with me If your | name be Barbara | Allen.
4. nigh him And | as she drew the | curtains back - Said "young | man I think you're | dying.
5. better Un - | til I have the | love of one The | love of Barbara | Allen."

The Cruel War

FINGER STRUM NO. 2

ARPEGGIO #2

1. The cruel war is rag - ing John - ny has to fight; I ___ want to be with him from morn - ing til night. _____

		G	Em	Am	Bm B7
2. I	want to be	with him. It	grieves my heart	so. Won't you
3. To	morrow is	Sunday	Monday is the	day - that your
4. Your	captain will	call you, it	grieves my heart	so. Won't you
5. I'll	tie back my	hair; Men's	clothing I'll put	on, I'll
6. I'll	pass as your	comrade, No	one will ever	know. Won't you
7. Oh	Johnny, oh	Johnny, I	fear you are un -	kind, I
8. I	love you far	better than	words can e'er ex -	press, won't you

		C	Am	G C	G
2.	let me go	with you?	No, my love	no.
3.	captain will	call you. And	you must o -	bey.
4.	let me go	with you?	No, my love	no.
5.	pass as your	comrade As	we march a -	long.
6.	let me go	with you?	No, my love	no.
7.	love you far	better. Than	all of man -	kind
8.	let me go	with you?	Yes, my love	yes.

Frankie And Johnny

PLUCKING STRUM

FINGER STRUM NO. 8

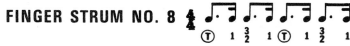

Frank-ie and John-ny were lov-ers, Oh, Lord-y how they could love. They swore to be true to each

oth - er. True as the stars a - bove. He was her man, but he done her wrong.

A				A7	D
2. Frankie went down to the	corner,	Just for a bucket of	beer.	said, "Oh Mister Bar -
3. "Don't want to cause you no	trouble,	Don't want to tell you no	lie, But	I saw your lover half an

			A		E7		A
tender, Has my	lovin' Johnny been	here? He is my	man,	and he wouldn't do	wrong."
hour a-go with a	gal named Nellie	Bly. He is your	man,	but he done you	wrong."

Santy Anno

FINGER STRUM NO. 12

PULL/BRUSH

(VERSE)

Am ... G C G ... Am ... G

1. We're sail-ing cross the riv-er from Liv-er-pool Heave a-way. Sant-y An-no

Dm ... G Em ... Am Em ... Am

'round Cape Horn to Fris-co Bay way___ out in Cal-i-for-ni-o. So

(CHORUS)

Am ... G C G ... Am ... G

heave her up and a-way we'll go heave a-way, San-ty An-no.

Dm ... G Em ... Am Em ... Am

Heave her up and a-way we'll go, Way___ out in Cal-i-for-ni-o.

		Am G	C G	Am	G
2.		Back in the days of	forty-nine Heave a-	way, Santy	An-no.
3.	There's	plenty of gold so	I've been told Heave a-	way, Santy	An-no.

		Dm	G Em	Am Em	Am
2.		Back in the days of	good old times way	out in Cal-i-	for-ni-o. So *(Chorus)*
3.		Plenty of gold so	I've been told way	out in Cal-i-	for-ni-o. So *(Chorus)*

Michael, Row The Boat Ashore

FOLK STRUM NO. 12

MUTE   MUTE

*F#m   xx3111

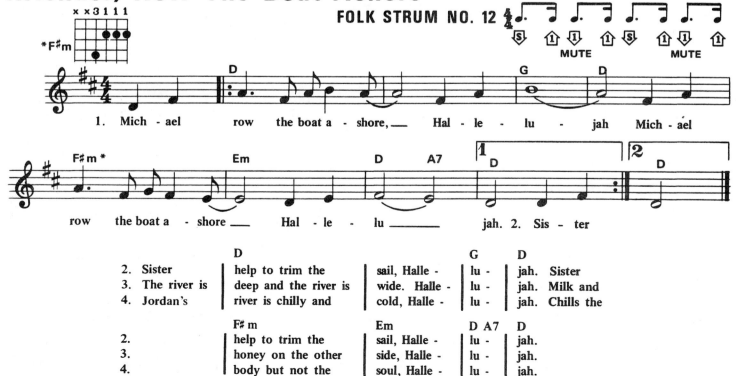

D

1. Mich-ael row the boat a-shore,___ Hal-le-lu-jah Mich-ael

F#m *   Em   D A7 |1 D |2 D

row the boat a-shore ___ Hal-le-lu _____ jah. 2. Sis-ter

		D		G	D	
2.	Sister	help to trim the		sail, Halle-	lu-	jah. Sister
3.	The river is	deep and the river is		wide. Halle-	lu-	jah. Milk and
4.	Jordan's	river is chilly and		cold, Halle-	lu-	jah. Chills the

		F#m		Em	D A7	D
2.		help to trim the		sail, Halle-	lu-	jah.
3.		honey on the other		side, Halle-	lu-	jah.
4.		body but not the		soul, Halle-	lu-	jah.

All My Trials

E.L. 2287

Jingle Bells

62
The First Noel

The __ First __ No - el the __ an - gels did say was to cer - tain poor

shep - herds in fields as they lay; in __ fields __ where __ they lay __ keep - ing their

sheep on a cold win - ter's night __ that was __ so deep. No - el, __ No -

el, No - el, No - el Born is the King __ of Is - re - al.

Silent Night

1. Si - lent night Ho - ly night all is calm

all is bright. Round yon vir - gin Moth - er and child.

Ho - ly In - fant so ten - der and mild. Sleep in Heav - en - ly

peace _____ Sleep __ in Heav - en - ly peace. _____

	A					E7	
2. Silent		night.		Holy		night.	Shepherds	quake

	A			D			A	
at the		sight.		Glories		stream from	Heaven a -	far,

	D			A			E7	
Heaven - ly		hosts sing,		Hallelu -		jah!	Christ, the	Saviour is

	A			E7		A	
born		/ / /		Christ, the	Saviour is	born.	/ / /

It Came Upon The Midnight Clear

FINGER STRUM NO. 12 PULL/BRUSH

It came u - pon___ the mid - night clear, That glor - i - ous

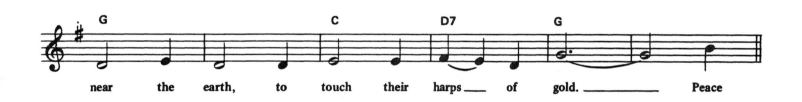

song ___ of old. _____ From an - gels bend - ing

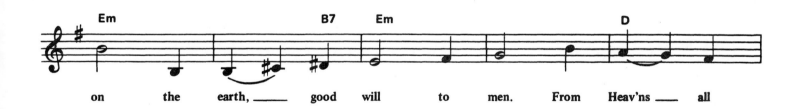

near the earth, to touch their harps___ of gold. _____ Peace

on the earth, ___ good will to men. From Heav'ns ___ all

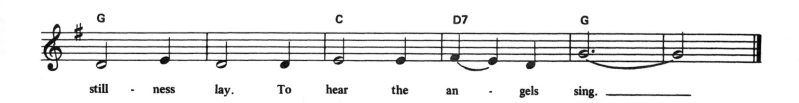

gra - cious King. _____ The world in sol - emn

still - ness lay. To hear the an - gels sing. _____

E.L. 2287

Song Index

Explanation of rating:

    E — *Easy* = only two or three chords with few changes

    M — *Medium* = easy chords but more frequent changes

    MD — *Medium-Difficult* = many chord changes, some bar chords

    D — *Difficult* = bar chords, frequent chord changes

E. L. 2287